Contents

Introduction

'Nobody wants a violent society, but we cannot leave it to chance. Building a non-violent society means an active commitment to non-violence.'

The Commission on Children and Violence

The aim of this book is to look at the many kinds of violence that exist in the world today. You may find some of the information upsetting. But you will also discover that there are many ways in which everyone can make a stand against violence whether it is in their own lives or in the lives of those around them, or by adding their voice to those working against violence worldwide.

Some of the focus of this book is on young people, because it is now understood that what happens to someone in their early years determines later attitudes towards violence.

Violence – what is it?

A violent mood

We have all known someone in a violent mood. We recognize tightly controlled anger, and we have seen anger that has been allowed to explode. You may know an adult whose behaviour is frightening in this way. You may have seen toddlers throwing violent tantrums before they have learnt to express their needs more effectively. Perhaps you have seen someone drunk in the street, yelling and threatening, with everyone keeping out of his or her way.

Seeing someone behave in a violent way can be frightening.

As you read this book, you may be surprised at how many kinds of violence there are. It seems that violence is everywhere. Some of the facts are difficult to accept, and you will discover that there are people living in violent situations that are hard even to imagine. But it is also important to remember that millions of people are working to combat violence in all its forms. We can all do something – take action, speak out and stand up for our own and other people's rights. At the end of this book you will find lots of ideas on how you can help make the world a less violent place.

VIOLENCE

Bridget Lawless

www.heinemann.co.uk
Visit our website to find out more information about **Heinemann Library** books.

To order:
 Phone 44 (0) 1865 888066
Send a fax to 44 (0) 1865 314091
Visit the Heinemann Bookshop at www.heinemann.co.uk to browse our catalogue
and order online.

First published in Great Britain by Heinemann Library, Halley Court, Jordan Hill, Oxford OX2 8EJ,
a division of Reed Educational and Professional Publishing Ltd.
Heinemann is a registered trademark of Reed Educational & Professional Publishing Limited.

OXFORD MELBOURNE AUCKLAND
JOHANNESBURG BLANTYRE GABORONE
IBADAN PORTSMOUTH NH (USA) CHICAGO

Designed by Tinstar Design (www.tinstar.co.uk)
Illustrations by Oxford Illustrators
Originated by Ambassador Litho Ltd
Printed by Wing King Tong in Hong Kong

ISBN 0 431 03533 4 (hardback)   ISBN 0 431 03538 5 (paperback)
04 03 02 01 00   04 03 02 01 00
10 9 8 7 6 5 4 3 2   10 9 8 7 6 5 4 3 2 1

British Library Cataloguing in Publication Data

Lawless, Bridget
        Violence. – (What's at issue)
        1. Violence – Juvenile literature 2. Interpersonal conflict –
        Juvenile literature
        I. Title
        303.6

Acknowledgements

The Publishers would like to thank the following for permission to reproduce photographs: Allsport
p 4/David Cannon p 23; Bubbles/Pauline Cutler pp 26, 33; Mary Evans Picture Library p 8; Corbis
pp 9, 11, 16, 41; Sally & Richard Greenhill p 38; Kobal Collection p 20/Richard Foreman p 5; Popperfoto
p 22/Yannis Behrakis p 12; Rex Features pp 14, 21, 39/Tim cowdry p 18 Craig Easton p 15/Simon Kleitem p 17/Sipa
p 13; Science Photo Library p 10; The Stockmarket/Roy Morsch p 32; Tony Stone Images/David Ash p 6/Cameron
Davidson p 24; Trip & Ast Directors/Grant p 36,/Greenberg p 40/Viesti p 30.
Cover photograph reproduced with permission of Trevor Clifford Photography

Our thanks to Julie Turner (School Counsellor, Banbury School, Oxfordshire) for her comments in the preparation of
this book.

Any words appearing in the text in bold, **like this**, are explained in the Glossary.

What is violence?

Dictionaries describe violence in different ways, but most agree that it is unjustified, excessive force. It can be a deliberate and intentional act by one person (the **perpetrator**) against another (the **victim**). It can also describe the behaviour of a crowd. It can apply to the content of a book, film or game, or describe a way of communicating. In fact, violence describes a wide range of **aggressive** actions, from arguments that get out of hand to **physical**, **sexual** or **emotional abuse**, from riots and **terrorism** to **torture** and war.

Is violence always physical?

On a person-to-person level, violence may involve physical injury such as hitting, fighting, cutting and bruising. It may result in serious injury or even death. However, it does not have to be extreme to be seen as an assault for which the perpetrator might be **prosecuted** by law.

'Do what you're told and no one will get hurt.' The gun may not even be loaded, but the threat of violence is often used by criminals to get victims to co-operate – as shown by these gangsters in the film *Point Break*.

In fact, even the threat of violence can be a criminal offence.

Violence can also be emotional or **psychological**. There may be no cuts or bruises to show, but a person can be mentally injured to the point where they are permanently damaged by repeated cruelty or threats, or by witnessing violence to others.

Violence can involve **coercion** – forcing someone to submit to something they are unwilling to do. This is often the case in armed robbery or **sexual assaults**, where the victim co-operates to reduce the risk of injury or threat to their life.

What causes it?

Violence can be triggered by many different kinds of situation and emotion. It may be a reaction to an event or situation that makes a person angry. It may be caused by the effects of drugs, alcohol or **hormones**, or it may be an inability to understand and control painful feelings.

Violence is sometimes a response to very stressful situations such as poor living conditions, unemployment, a broken relationship or the strain of living in poverty. Using violence might make a person who feels helpless feel more powerful and in control. Some people express their **frustration** with others by being violent instead of talking about their problems or trying to **negotiate** their differences of opinion.

Naturally violent?

There is no real proof that anyone is born violent. However, experts believe there may be something in a person's **genetic** make-up (their inherited characteristics) that, combined with negative influences, could make violent behaviour more likely. By negative influences we mean unpleasant experiences like a violent upbringing or very severe **humiliation** by a teacher or other adult in a position of authority.

Maybe he did not like the other man's driving, maybe the traffic is getting on his nerves, but that's no excuse for the aggressive behaviour we now call **road rage**.

Mental illness – a minor factor

It is estimated that about 5–10 per cent of violent people have a physical or mental condition that causes or contributes to their behaviour. They may need treatment in a **psychiatric** hospital or, if they have committed a violent crime, they may be sent to a special prison where they can receive medical or psychiatric care.

Strength in numbers

Some people are more likely to behave in a violent manner when they are in a group than when they are on their own. Belonging to a gang might mean being expected to fight or show aggression to rival gang members.

Driven to violence

People who are normally law-abiding and quiet may become violent in the face of injustice. A group protesting quietly about job losses or pay cuts might start fighting with riot police who want them to move on. In countries where people have little freedom and no opportunity to vote against brutal leaders, citizens may resort to violence to remove those leaders from power.

THE CYCLE OF VIOLENCE

It is now widely recognized that violence is often part of a cycle of learnt behaviour. A person who is a victim of violence, particularly over a period of time, is much more likely to become violent themselves. Millions of young people witness, or are subjected to, violence at an early age in the home. They may copy that behaviour by fighting or **bullying** others at school. Later, violence may be a feature of their adult relationships. When they have children, they may treat them with violence, and those children may also witness violence between the parents. So the destructive cycle continues. This is why tackling violence, even at an early age – so breaking the cycle wherever it occurs, is seen as the vital key to a less violent world.

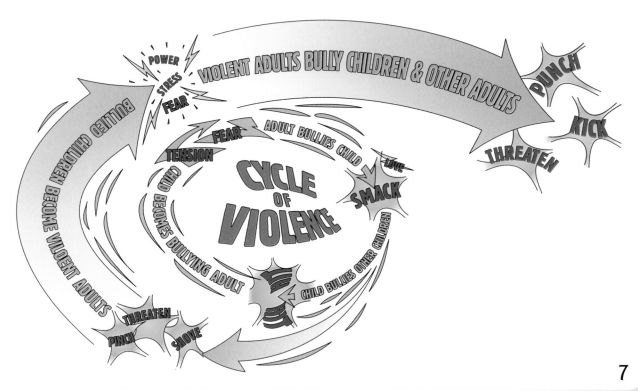

7

Is the world a more violent place today?

The world has always been a violent place and people have often had to fight to survive. Humans are unique as a species in that we **torture**, fight and kill even when our survival does not depend on it. Violence is often driven by greed, or the belief that one group of people is better than another.

Learning to be honest about our history

It is only quite recently that we have started to look at the history of the so-called '**civilized**' world more honestly. History books have always concealed or 'rewritten' facts about the violence of their own nation. For example, the

Violence can be concealed in the language we use to describe things. Calling black people 'savages' meant white people could ignore their feelings and their rights. This is an early 19th century engraving of a slave ship.

colonization of Africa, America, Asia and Australia by so-called 'civilized' white countries were in fact shamefully violent episodes of human history. White invaders considered the native people to be primitive or dangerously savage. Black people were made slaves, whipped and chained and treated as property. They were even hunted and shot for sport.

In the **Nazi** era of the Second World War, more than six million Jewish men, women and children were brutally murdered by the

STREET CHILDREN

In many places, violence is an inescapable reality that children and the less well-off live with every day. In Latin America, parts of Asia and the Indian subcontinent, **street children** are a common sight. In some parts of Europe they are appearing too, as children flee from the conflicts of Eastern Europe. Today, there are an estimated 100 million children worldwide living on the streets. Some are orphans, some have been rejected, deserted or abandoned, but most have run away from families who cannot take care of them properly. Street children have to look after themselves, living off rubbish, trying to earn money by odd jobs. Many are sexually mistreated by adults, **raped**, beaten and sold for sex. They cannot turn to the police for help because the police often do the same things to them. In some Latin American countries, street children are rounded up and imprisoned or killed, just to tidy up the streets for an important foreign visitor.

Unloved, unwanted, unable to trust adults – survival is an endless battle and violence an everyday reality for the world's street children, as shown here in India.

Germans – simply because they did not fit the Nazi racial ideal. In Eastern Europe and on almost every continent of the world today, people continue to terrify, torture and kill people who belong to other **ethnic groups** – and claim to have 'good reason' to do so.

Do we live in particularly violent times?

Although we like to think of ourselves as more civilized than ever, violence is still everywhere we look. This is partly because 24-hour television news brings us endless images of violent events from all over the world. We can witness violence, bombings and other **atrocities** even as they are happening.

Fear of violence

Many people in the **developed world** are afraid of being attacked on the street or in their own home. Parents today are less willing to let children play out of sight or travel alone because the world is seen as a less safe place.

War

Whatever the reason for which wars are fought, they are always violent and bloody. The weapons of war are intended to inflict terrible injury and death in order to destroy the enemy or make them surrender.

Over thousands of years, weapons have developed from simple clubs, spears and slings, into cannons, guns, rockets and bombs. Advances in science and technology have generated new kinds of warfare that enable the greatest amount of damage to be done from the furthest distance. Weapons of mass destruction, such as nuclear bombs, are capable of destroying all life and property within a radius of many kilometres, leaving the area **contaminated** with **radiation** for years to come. Chemical weapons can cause terrible burns and attack the nervous system, lungs and eyes. **Bacteria** and **viruses** are used in germ warfare to spread disease that kills the population or makes them too sick to fight.

PSYCHOLOGICAL EFFECTS

Soldiers are not immune to the horrors of war either. Increasingly, in Western countries, soldiers returning from combat are seeking professional help and **counselling**, and are speaking out about the effects of their experiences.

More than a quarter of a million people were estimated to have died when nuclear bombs destroyed the Japanese cities of Hiroshima and Nagasaki in 1945. Thousands more suffered the terrible long-term effects of radiation sickness.

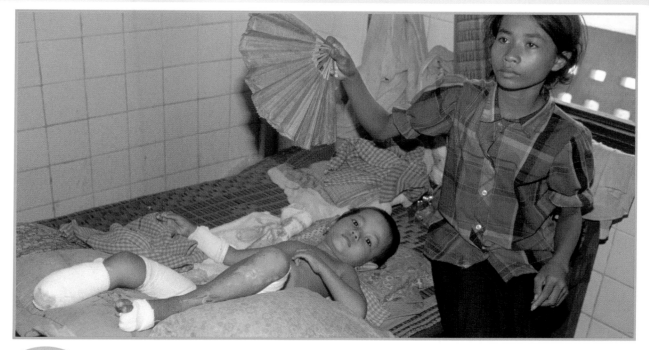

Landmines target not only soldiers, but civilians (including children), aid workers and animals. These weapons continue to kill and maim even years after a war is over.

Who gets hurt?

The 'rules' of war say that soldiers are supposed to fight soldiers, but the number of **civilian** casualties is estimated to have risen from 5 to 90 per cent in recent decades, with women and children the main targets. Some are caught in the cross-fire, others are injured or killed in bombing raids or by **landmines**. Those who are taken prisoner may face **torture**, **rape** or death.

A war on hearts and minds

The **psychological** effects of war can be as devastating as the physical ones. People who witness the **massacre** of their loved ones or even their entire community suffer deep psychological damage. For these people, who are homeless, starving and in fear of their lives, there is no chance to **grieve** normally.

Children in war

Millions of children worldwide are caught up in wars. In the past twenty years, an estimated two million children have been killed in armed conflict. Another six million have been seriously injured or permanently disabled, often by landmines. Hundreds of thousands of children have lived their entire life in the midst of war, exposed to relentless violence and terror. The only games some of these children know are based on what they witness every day, for example, gun fighting, bombs and people being blown up.

CHILD SOLDIERS

At least 250,000 children, some under ten years old, are fighting in wars today. Some are volunteers, but many have been kidnapped at a young age and prepared for war, not only by combat training but by exposure to extreme violence that numbs their normal reactions. They may even be forced to kill members of their own family and community.

Hope against war and violence

Refugees

Every year, millions of people flee to another land because of war, or because they fear death, **persecution** or **torture** in their own country.

When a refugee arrives in another country, they may seek **asylum** – safe refuge – there. They have to establish that they face persecution or death if they are sent home, but that is often very difficult to prove. They may be held in detention for years until a decision is made about them or they can be housed. For thousands of refugees, it is the start of a new life. It is a chance to recover from the terrors of torture or war. For some, it is also a vital opportunity to tell the world what is really happening in the country they have fled, so that those left behind will one day receive help.

> **FACT**
>
> *There are an estimated 27.4 million refugees and 30 million displaced people worldwide. At least 50% are children.*

Refugees risk all trying to escape from war, persecution or death in their own country. These Kosovan Albanian refugees fled to neighbouring countries when forced to leave their homes by the Serbs in former Yugoslavia.

Working against violence and war

Many organizations work to expose injustice in hard-hitting worldwide campaigns. They challenge governments about ill-treatment of people and publish information about **violations** of human rights all over the world. Dedicated people risk imprisonment or even death in order to get information to those who can use it most effectively.

Individuals suffering torture or imprisonment because of their nationality, political beliefs or religion sometimes become the focus of specific campaigns. If they are lucky, they get to hear that people are working on their behalf, or will even receive letters of support. Imagine being alone, shackled to a damp wall in an isolated cell, and learning one day that thousands of people you have never met are working to win your freedom!

Never giving up

For 27 years Nelson Mandela, leader of the **African National Congress**, was held as a political prisoner in South Africa. Throughout the struggle for black equality and the end of **apartheid**, Nelson Mandela's leadership inspired millions of people worldwide. The world's most famous prisoner was elected President of South Africa four years after his release, at the age of 75.

In Burma, Nobel Peace Prize winner and **National Democratic Party** leader Aung San Suu Kyi has been under house arrest since 1989 – she has been an official prisoner in her own home, with occasional releases and sudden re-arrests. Despite winning the 1990 Burmese election, her rightful leadership is not recognized by the power-holding military regime, who are also accused of serious human rights abuses against their own people. Some countries have imposed trading bans until the Burmese government end their brutal treatment of citizens and accept democratic reform.

Aung Sun Suu Kyi's quiet dignity and unshakeable certainty that her country will one day be free from military rule has been an inspiration to her millions of followers.

Terrorism

After 30 years of violent religious and social conflict, the Northern Ireland peace talks seemed at last to have succeeded in 1998.

Terrorists are people who use violence, or the threat of it, to bring attention to a cause they feel strongly about. This may be intended to inform people, or make people fearful of what could happen if their demands are not met.

Terrorist acts include bombing public places, important buildings or transport, or hijacking planes at gun point. Terrorists may kidnap people or take over a building where people are working and hold them against their will. Their **victims** are subjected to terror and some may be

However, extremists tried to halt the process with a bomb that killed and maimed hundreds of people in a quiet Omagh shopping centre.

killed to prove that the terrorists mean business. Some terrorists are wealthy, influential people who send others to do their work, and can afford to fund their own armies and weapon supplies.

Terrorists often try to demand that a government or group agrees to release certain prisoners. They may demand money, political freedoms or safe passage. Most governments refuse to give in to their demands as it will make **terrorism** seem an attractive route for other **extremists**.

John McCarthy Freed!

KASHMIR HOSTAGES FEARED DEAD

UN Hostages to be Released

Chechnya Hostages Alive and Well

Hostages

Terrorists often take hostages who are from a country that they believe they can influence. People working or travelling in certain countries may get caught up in a political struggle that does not involve them, but which changes their own and their families' lives forever.

Hostages may be held for days, months or many years. They may be kept blindfolded and tied up with no idea where they are. Their days are filled with misery. Every change in routine is frightening… Why are they being moved? Has something happened? Are they going to be killed? Naturally, such an ordeal can be mentally damaging, and the conditions they are kept in take a terrible toll on their health. While their families and friends campaign for their release, the hostages can only hope and pray that they are not forgotten and that one day they will be set free.

Messages from hostages are precious signs of life for waiting families, but nothing is a greater relief than that prayed for reunion. The journalist John McCarthy was released after 5 years in captivity.

Violent protest

Fighting for rights, fighting against wrongs

People protest when they feel strongly about something. It is a way of objecting about a proposed change or innovation (such as a new road), or expressing anger and frustration with how things are. Protest is a way of taking power, of 'doing something about it', rather than meekly accepting what the government, big business or a foreign power wants to impose.

In countries where people have basic rights of free expression, anyone can join in a peaceful protest march or meeting. Some people believe that the only way to get attention for a cause is by showing how angry they are, which turns a protest into a riot. The police have a duty to try to contain the protesting group and prevent conflict. Unfortunately, both rioters and police sometimes respond with more violence. In such a clash, both police and rioters may be seriously hurt or killed.

Crushing those who speak out

Where people do not enjoy the freedom to express their opinions, they may be beaten, shot or imprisoned for trying to speak out. Their own police or army might use violence to break up protesting groups. In South Africa, during the worst years of **apartheid**, thousands of black people, including hundreds of children and youths, were killed or injured while fighting for their freedom. In 1989, in China's Tiananmen Square, hundreds of protesting students were killed when the government crushed their demand for democracy.

When protesters and police clash, each blames the other for starting the trouble. Protesters and police now use video cameras to gather evidence of what really happens.

RACISM

Race issues have been the cause of hundreds of violent clashes and many highly organized groups still try to incite violence and hatred towards black people, religious groups and foreigners. In the southern states of the USA, the **Ku Klux Klan** believe that white Protestants are superior to black people and other religious groups. In South Africa, supporters of apartheid continue to believe that they should have more rights than black people. In Britain, the National Front is an extreme **racist** political party. Modern-day Nazi groups in Germany and elsewhere in Europe continue to believe in the racist ideals that led to the murder of millions of Jews when Hitler was in power.

Non-violent protest

Peaceful protest has always been a way of getting opinion across, and has an important role to play in the fight against war, weapons and violent destruction. In recent years, peaceful protest has developed into increasingly organized systems of **non-violent** confrontation. So-called **eco warriors** take their name from the mainly **ecological** issues that they fight for. Road-building programmes and the proposed destruction of sites of scientific interest or natural beauty bring eco warriors into action.

Well-equipped and prepared for a long wait, they build tree houses and walkways, establish ground camps and dig underground tunnels. These are all designed to prevent the destruction they oppose from ever getting under way. While the eco warriors fight the developers in the law courts, the developers come with eviction orders and police support to throw the protesters out. Eco warriors chain themselves to blocks of concrete, lock themselves in booby-trapped tunnels and camp out in trees that are going to be cut down. All these strategies delay the developers' work and help play for time.

Eco warriors' skills of non-violent protest have been developed and adopted by protesters all over the world. However, non-violent strategies can sometimes still put protesters on the wrong side of the law.

Violence towards animals

While it is reasonably easy to get everyone to agree that violence by one person to another is wrong, when it comes to violence towards animals there is a wide range of bitterly opposed opinions. In a few countries the way animals are reared in farms and the suffering of live animals being transported for slaughter abroad are the subject of anti-cruelty laws.

FACT

Many people who feel strongly about animal welfare believe it is wrong to rear animals for food and that farming methods cause suffering to animals. Some people choose to become vegetarian for this reason.

Bloodsports – fun for animals?

Many people are convinced that hunting foxes, stags, otters and other animals for sport is the best way of keeping their numbers down. They claim there is no particular suffering on the animals' part, either during the chase or at the kill. An equally outspoken lobby claims that **bloodsports** are cruel and unnecessary and certainly do cause the hunted animal distress before it is torn apart by the hounds. Anti-hunt demonstrators stage many peaceful protests, but some choose violence and personal attacks on hunters to try and get their message across.

Attempts to get laws passed to ban all hunting have repeatedly failed. However, in the UK, a study claiming that deer suffer stress during hunts resulted in the National Trust banning deer hunts on all its land. (The National Trust is a charity that owns and preserves thousands of acres of natural beauty.) Hunting is an issue that will cause violent disagreement for years to come.

Fighting for their lives

Dog fights are an illegal form of gambling. People bet on dogs that are made to fight until one is too badly injured to continue, or is even killed. Sometimes even the winning animal's injuries are so bad it has to be put down. Similarly, bull-fighting is considered a form of entertainment, and tourists flock to bull rings in Spain to witness the slow slaughter of a bull in a matador's ritual performance.

Some say fox hunting is sport, and others say it's cruelty.

Laboratory experiments – science or suffering?

Using animals to test the safety of cosmetics has now been banned in Britain. While it is widely agreed that animals should not have to suffer unnecessarily, millions of animals are used every day in scientific experiments. Cats, dogs, monkeys, pigs, rats, mice and other species are specially bred for the purpose and know only pain in their short lives. Many undergo operations without anaesthetic, have their skulls opened, are given shocks, poisons and diseases, and are killed when they are no longer useful.

Some scientists believe these experiments are justified in the search for knowledge and medical cures. Others believe such experiments are **unethical**, unnecessary and give unreliable results. While supporters of animal rights campaign for changes in the law, some protesters use violence to punish and try to stop the experimenters, because animals can't fight for themselves. But can violence ever be the answer?

1 That's the third letter bomb in a fortnight. It's great. The Animal Guardians are really giving those lab workers a taste of their own medicine.

I don't agree with it. You can't fight violence with violence.

2 This is the only thing that will make them listen. Animal experiments have to be stopped. I'm going to join Guardians today.

I don't like animal experiments either, but it's not that simple – and more violence isn't the answer.

3 I take medicines that were tested on animals. I wouldn't be able to live without them, I'd always be in pain. I haven't got the right to attack scientists who are trying to help people like me – or to stop the development of drugs that could help someone else.

4 I hadn't thought about that. But ... you love animals, and they can't defend themselves.

You're right. And I should be doing something to change things. There are plenty of people who say these experiments aren't necessary. But I just don't think bombs are the way.

5 Then let's find a group that's working for the same thing without violence, and join that.

Yes – I bet there are scientists who feel the same too.

The media

Violent images and story-lines frequently appear in films, videos and computer games. Experts simply do not agree over whether anyone, including young people, will be badly influenced by seeing images of fighting, murder and horror, or by watching extreme material, such as a so-called 'video nasty'.

Some people think that media violence may lead to copy-cat behaviour or make viewers less sensitive to violence. They argue that young minds are even more likely to be influenced than those of adults. Of course, it is impossible to know whether this is true, without making young people watch extreme material and waiting to see what happens later in their lives. On the other hand, we have all

Violent scenes in films, video and television may often be portayed as being funny.

seen playground replays of fights and chases that were on television the night before. Even pre-school children mimic the kicks and punches of their television super-heroes.

The risk of young people copying screen violence is not the only issue. In a lot of films, television drama and videos, children are shown as the **victims** of adults, and women as the victims of men. This is seen as reinforcing those negative roles in society. Perhaps most worrying of all is the fact that violence is often made into a form of entertainment and may be portrayed as being funny.

ACTING OUT WHAT THEY'VE SEEN?

In 1994, the debate about media violence suddenly came into the limelight. Two ten year-old boys abducted two year-old James Bulger from a busy shopping centre in England and brutally murdered him. The fact that the boys had recently been watching violent 'video nasties' was thought – but could not be proven – to have influenced the crime.

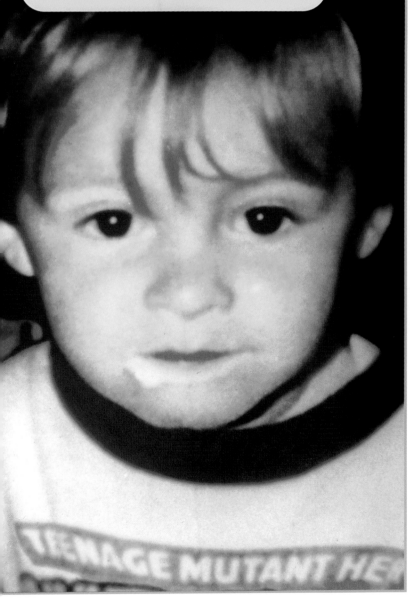

Protecting viewers from violence – in theory

Television broadcasters increasingly accept that they have a duty to educate. This affects how they portray violence and victims. In the UK, broadcasters are also bound by guidelines that put strict limits on showing violence and bad language before the so-called evening 'watershed' hour, after which stronger material can be shown.

Many countries use certification categories to control admission to films that may contain violence or bad language. Because young people can get access to videos more easily, these are more tightly censored. Videos are not only given a certificate but more extreme scenes are cut entirely. Each country decides its own limits on what may or may not be seen and by which age group. Some countries impose no controls at all.

Computer games – toys for the boys?

Whether violent computer games have a bad influence on young people is also hotly debated. Critics complain that there is hardly anything other than violent games to buy and that too many games show women as victims and foreigners as 'baddies'.

Sport

Everyone who has played a team sport knows that games can get rough. But some critics fear that in professional sport, violence is becoming part of the game itself.

Bad behaviour on the pitch

With fans urging players to tackle each other and thousands of people shouting encouragement or insults, it is hardly surprising that the temperature sometimes rises on the pitch. Some players are better at blocking out anything that might wind them up – whether it comes from their fans or opponents. Others play back to the audience, showing off their good humour – or their bad temper. Some players are simply on a short fuse and if they are put under pressure they easily lose control.

So why are such players tolerated, especially in games watched by millions of young people as well as adults? The main reason is money. Great footballers bring in the fans and earn their club big rewards. Sometimes, a hot temper is mistaken for a colourful personality, drawing in publicity and extra press coverage. Violence on the pitch can hurt in more ways than one...

A display of temper cost David Beckham his fans' respect and probably lost England's chance of reaching the quarter finals of the 1998 World Cup, although Diego Simeoni later admitted exaggerating his reaction.

Fans running wild

Football hooligans cause terror and damage before, during and after matches, often having consumed large quantities of alcohol. Innocent fans and local residents are frequently caught up in the violence of a dangerous minority who arm themselves with bottles, bricks and knives and go looking for trouble. Often fights are arranged in advance, so special police officers work undercover pretending to be fans. They join the organized fighting groups so that they can get information about ring leaders and send advance warning to local police squads where fights are planned.

Boxing – sport or violence?

Despite its enormous popularity as a spectator sport, boxing has come under heavy criticism in recent years. Unlike most sports, in boxing the competitors' aim is to injure each other. Unsurprisingly, a high number of boxers have been left permanently injured, brain damaged or blind. Twenty professional boxers have died after fights as a result of their injuries in the last ten years.

A growing international body of doctors, individuals and organizations are calling for professional boxing to be banned and for young people to be prevented from ever practising the sport. In countries like the UK where a doctor has to be present at every fight by law, it has been suggested that doctors could effectively put a halt to the boxing by refusing to attend fights.

INSULT OR INJURY

Boxer Mike Tyson was fined $3 million and had his licence suspended for biting a piece out of Evander Holyfield's ear during a fight. Many felt Tyson should have been banned from the ring forever.

Violent fans are an international headache for football clubs, the police and the general public. A group of Liverpool and Juventus fans during the 1985 European Cup Final.

Boys – more violent than girls?

It is often said that violence is a male problem. This is because a far higher number of boys and men use violence compared with girls and women. Of course there are violent females – girls who fight, women who abuse their children or partners, or even commit murder – but the numbers are very small compared to the number of violent males.

Some experts say the causes are **social**. They claim boys are treated differently from an early age. Boys are told not to cry when they hurt themselves, but to stand up for themselves and fight back. They are not encouraged to talk about or show their feelings, so anger and **frustration** are expressed in other ways. Macho images (men are shown as tough and strong, like many movie heroes for example) are also blamed for creating violent role models.

More men than women may use violence, but that does not mean all males are violent. Many men and boys believe in peaceful living and some devote their lives to opposing violence in all its forms.

Many social factors, such as poor housing, living in a single parent family and bad schooling are blamed for or used to explain away male **aggression**. But none of those situations are exclusively male. Girls growing up with the same disadvantages do not become violent in anything like the same numbers.

Some experts claim that violence is a natural and important part of male behaviour, dating back to the days when men were hunters and had to protect women and children from both wild animals and other males. Women argue that even if that were the case, such behaviour has no place in the modern world and men must learn to adapt.

The cycle of violence

Many boys and men are caught up in the cycle of violence and are so used to hitting and being hit, or using their strength to get what they want, that they never learn more appropriate ways of dealing with people. Later, they are likely to surround themselves with men who have a similar, equally violent outlook. This reinforces their certainty that such behaviour is right. Violence breeds violence.

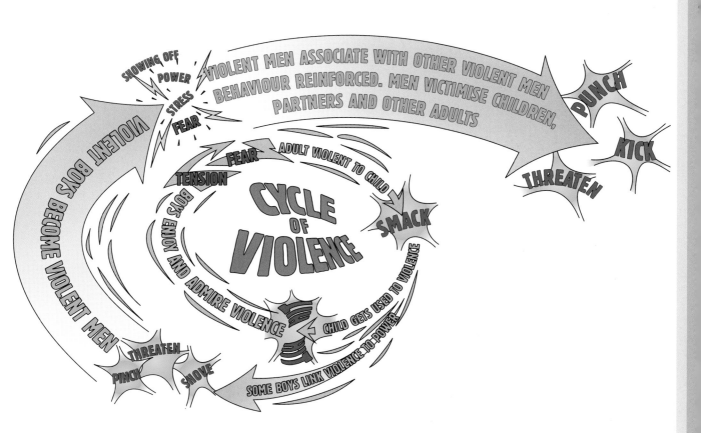

Bullying

What do we mean by bullying?

Bullying is a deliberate kind of power abuse, often repeated over a period of time, in which the bully **humiliates**, frightens, threatens or physically hurts their **victim**. Bullies tend to pick on people who cannot defend themselves well and often encourage others to join in.

Bullying can be
- PHYSICAL: hitting, kicking, pinching and taking or damaging the victim's belongings or demanding money
- VERBAL: calling names, insulting, making **racist** remarks or cruel comments
- INDIRECT: spreading nasty stories about the victim, ignoring or excluding them from **social** groups and activities.

Being bullied

It is estimated that at least a quarter of primary school children and about 10 per cent of secondary school children are bullied at some time. Most tell no one what is happening to them and bullies are careful to ensure that adults do not see what they are up to.

FACT

Between 1997 and 1998 nearly 20,000 young people called the UK phoneline, ChildLine, for help and advice about bullying. (See page 46 for details on ChildLine.) Nearly 75% were girls. Were there fewer boys being bullied, or do girls find it easier to seek help?

How does it feel?

A person being bullied will probably feel very alone and frightened of places or situations where they know the bully is likely to seek them out or attack them. Both their school work and their confidence will probably suffer. Some victims of bullying may be driven to suicide. The note they leave may be the first anyone else knows of what they had been going through.

Why does someone become a bully?

Bullies may be strong, confident people who enjoy showing off their control over others. More often, they are quite

Bullies rely on three things: that no one tells, that no one stands up for the victim and that no one steps in if the victim seeks help.

insecure people who feel more powerful if they can put someone else down. Some bullies are jealous of their victim or something the victim can do well. Bullies are sometimes simply displaying negative attitudes learnt from their parents, for example by expressing racist views or by picking on people who are different in some way.

School bullying policies

Every school should have a policy on bullying that makes it clear bullying is not acceptable and spells out the steps that will be taken when bullying incidents are discovered. Some schools tackle the problem by trying to help the bully understand how it feels to be bullied, or by making the bully face their actions in front of their class. The aim is to stop the bullying and help both bully and victim regain self respect.

ACTION

No adult or child has the right to bully anyone else.

- If you are being bullied it is important to talk to a responsible adult.
- If the bullying does not stop, tell again, or talk to another adult.
- If you are a bully, stop and think what it may feel like to be bullied.

THE CYCLE OF VIOLENCE

Many bullies have been bullied themselves in the past, or are living with violence at home. A very high proportion of young people who are later convicted of offences are also ex-bullies, or were victims of bullying.

FACT

It is estimated that one young person commits suicide every month because of bullying in the UK. If you need help for yourself or a friend, or want to find out more about what you and your school can do to tackle bullying, try using BULLYING as a keyword search on the Internet. Or check out bullying from the menu on the Childline web site at http://www.childline.org.uk

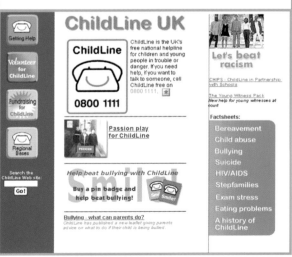

Forced to be a bully

29

Domestic violence

Domestic violence is any kind of violence that happens in the family or home. It is found in virtually all societies, as much in the **developing world** as in industrialized countries. It makes no difference what race, class or religion the family is, whether they are wealthy or poor, or whether home is a castle, house, apartment or refugee camp. Domestic violence can happen anywhere.

Figures about family violence can never be accurate because it happens behind closed doors. It has been estimated that one in four women is living in a violent relationship and it is thought that between half and two-thirds of men who beat their wives also beat their children. Occasionally, men are also victims of violent female partners or both partners are as violent as each other.

Why don't domestic violence victims leave their violent partners?

There are lots of reasons why someone will stay in a violent relationship. Leaving someone you love is never easy. Many violent men are very sorry about what they have done to their partner or children afterwards and make promises to change. Women are often ashamed of what is happening to them or won't admit it to themselves. They may conceal not only their own bruises, but their children's, too.

In the **developed world**, more and more women have the courage and freedom to leave violent partners. In many cultures escaping from domestic violence is very difficult because women are economically dependent or may become outcasts if they leave their partner.

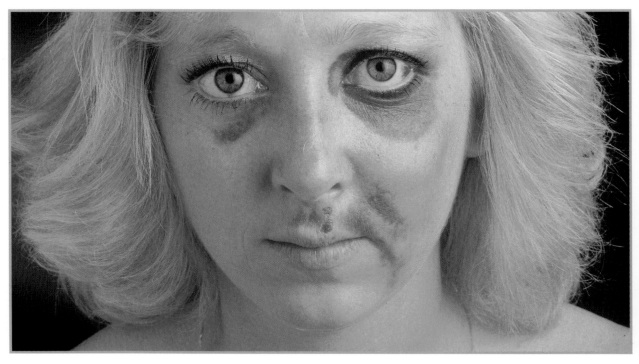

The cycle of violence

Those who have known violence as children may become **repeat victims**, who associate violence with love. They may be drawn to violent partners partly for this reason. Although there can be an element of choice in remaining with a violent partner, that does not mean the violence is the victim's fault.

Victims of domestic violence are increasingly encouraged to report assaults. Many countries now have special police Domestic Violence Units with officers trained to deal with family conflict. However, women who say they want to press assault charges often change their minds later. They may fear breaking up the family and losing their home, financial support and what little security they have. For those who choose to leave, women's refuge networks worldwide provide safe places for women and children to make a new start.

FACT

A National Society for the Prevention of Cruelty to Children (NSPCC) campaign highlighted that violence in the home is not acceptable and encouraged young people to speak out. If you are forced to live with violence, tell someone now or seek help from one of the organizations listed at the back of this book.

FACT

Hundreds of women are in prison for killing violent husbands or partners. Supporters campaign for their freedom, claiming that the women had lived for years in fear of their lives and that their actions were not pre-planned murders but self-defence. Many such women are released every year on appeal.

Abuse

'Don't talk to strangers'

Children have traditionally been warned to be wary of strangers, but in fact children and young people are far more at risk of being **physically**, **sexually** or **emotionally abused**, or even murdered, by a family member than by a stranger.

ABUSE

- Emotional abuse is mistreatment that causes a person emotional damage or **psychological** harm.
- Physical abuse is threatening or actually injuring someone by hitting, punching, smacking or other physical means.
- Sexual abuse is harmful touching or hurting of someone in a sexual way, or forcing them to perform sexual acts.

FACT

Separate studies in the UK, USA and Australia found that 60% of child murder victims were killed by their own parents. In societies where boys are more valued than girls, parents sometimes deliberately kill their girl babies.

For millions of children and young people, the family is not a safe place.

Between 1997–8, the UK helpline **ChildLine** answered nearly 10,000 calls from young people reporting sexual abuse. (See page 46 for details on ChildLine). Fathers were abusing their own children more than any other category of abuser. In fact, in almost half the cases, it was a close male relative who was responsible for the abuse of the child. In over 12,000 calls about physical abuse, fathers were the **perpetrators** in nearly 40 per cent of cases and mothers just under 30 per cent.

Living with the fear of violence

But what is it like to be living day to day in a family where violence, or the threat of it, is a constant reality? Some children know no other life and have no real sense of a safe, stable and loving environment.

I dread Dad coming home in the evening. Especially if he's been drinking.

When Dad's around, everything changes. You can't make a noise or play. He just loses his temper.

I told Mum I didn't want to go to my uncle's any more. But she said I was being stupid. I'm too embarrassed to tell her he keeps touching me.

Mum can't seem to cope these days, she hits us for no reason at all.

Dad was hitting Mum. I shouted at him to stop, but he hit me and my little brother as well.

I'm scared when Dad comes into my room. I know he's going to do things to me and make me promise not to tell.

Somewhere to turn

Telling a responsible adult such as a parent, other relative, teacher or youth worker is the first step in stopping abuse. Some young people prefer to start by contacting a helpline. Each year, millions of young people take that first step by making **anonymous** contact with an adult who can help via special children's phonelines. Telling someone else that you are being physically or sexually abused can be very hard, especially as most young victims believe it is somehow their fault. They want the abuse to stop, but fear what will happen if they tell. The friendly voice on the end of the phoneline can explain that what has been happening is not the victim's fault and can guide them through their fears. This may eventually enable the victim to seek help from other adults around them.

Not all calls to helplines are from victims. Many young people call for advice because they are worried about a friend.

Telling someone is the first step to stopping the abuse. Helplines are often busy as other young people need to talk to someone, too. But don't give up – your call will be answered eventually. You could also try to think of other people around you who you can turn to for support if the helplines are busy.

FACT

ChildLine answered more than 100,000 calls in 1997–8. But an estimated 10,000 children a day – that's over 3 million a year – try to get through. These figures have highlighted the size of the problem and shown that a huge number of children are living with violence.

Breaking the silence

Twelve year-old Sasha decided to break the silence about abuse in her family. She chose to share what happened to her so that children in similar situations might have the courage to seek help.

(1)

My Dad sexually abused me since I was six. I loved him as my Dad, but I was also terrified of him and hated being alone with him. I knew what he was doing to me was wrong, but he told me he couldn't help it and that it was my fault because he loved me so much. I felt very dirty and ashamed and guilty because he made me keep a secret. He said I should never tell anyone because we would both get into trouble.

(2) I thought it was only me that was 'special' to Dad. Then when I was ten, I realized he was interested in my little brother and sister in the same way. I talked to them to find out if he was touching them in an inappropriate way or making them do things they didn't want to do. Like me, they were afraid to say anything at first but in the end they told me he'd hurt them too. That's when I knew if I didn't do something, they'd suffer for years just like I had.

(3)

I couldn't tell Mum, or anyone else I knew. I didn't think anyone would believe me. In the end I called a helpline. I'd seen the number on a poster at school. It took me three goes before I could even say anything, but the people who answered were very patient and kind. It was such a relief when I managed to say what was happening and how scared I was for my brother and sister.

4 They told me it wasn't my fault and that it was important to tell someone I could trust. I decided to tell a teacher I like at school first. I was very embarrassed and frightened, but she was really kind and helpful. She convinced me that we had to tell Social Services because my Dad was doing something very bad, and that they would talk to my Mum. We needed protection and Dad needed help.

5 Mum was very shocked and upset. She was angry with my Dad and with herself for not knowing we were being hurt. The woman from Social Services and the police came to my house. I was scared what would happen. Dad denied everything at first, but at the police station, he admitted what I'd said was true.

6 Dad had to go to court. He didn't go to prison but he's having special therapy. He's moved out of the house. I'm really sad that our family is broken up, but at last I feel safe. My brother and sister and I are all having counselling and I still cry about what happened. I still love my Dad and see him now and then, but he's not allowed to be with us alone. Dad broke everyone's trust and hurt everyone he loves. We've all lost something, but I know I did the right thing to tell and I know what happened wasn't my fault.

SOME SECRETS SHOULD BE TOLD. IF SOMEONE IS HURTING OR ABUSING YOU, SPEAK OUT!

A little smack

The question of whether adults have the right to smack young people has become a very hot issue in recent years. A growing body of opinion claims that as we all agree hitting adults is wrong, it surely must be wrong to hit children, too. Why should a child have fewer rights than an adult?

Anti-smacking campaigners believe rewarding good behaviour is the way to guide children away from danger, naughtiness or disobedience. Once smacking starts, they say, it has to continue because if the child doesn't learn, where does the smacking stop? They claim parents do not realize how hard they hit and that they conceal physical assault behind phrases like 'it was just a little smack' and 'I don't hit them, I only give them a tap'.

The shock of a smack may stop the tantrum, but will it teach good behaviour?

THE RIGHT TO BE PROTECTED FROM ILL-TREATMENT?

Britain says No, the EC says Yes
In 1994, a man who had repeatedly hit his 11 year-old stepson with a garden cane was charged with assault and **actual bodily harm**. His defence was that the beatings amounted to 'reasonable punishment', allowable under English law.

The jury let him off.
But the boy took his case to the European Court of Human Rights, (the highest legal court in Europe whose judgements can overrule those of member countries). He complained that the English law had failed to adequately protect him from ill-treatment by his stepfather. In 1998 the court agreed and awarded the boy £10,000 compensation and his legal costs.

The cycle of violence

Smacking and other forms of physical punishment are shown to play a part in the cycle of violence. Children who regard being hit as normal are more likely to hit out themselves against other children and, later in life, against other adults and their own children.

HEI! KĀORE TĀTOU E PATU TĀNGATA ANA I KONEI
HEY! WE DON'T HIT ANYBODY HERE
E! O TATOU UA FA'ASĀ ONA FASITAGATA I'INEI

End Physical Punishment of Children (EPOCH)

A major campaign was launched in the UK in 1989 to help organizations all over the world try to end the physical punishment of children and to find **non-violent** ways of raising children. The campaigners say that it is time to end physical punishment of children worldwide because:

- hitting children is a **violation** of their fundamental rights as people and a constant confirmation of their low status;

All over the world, there are moves to make hitting children unacceptable or actually against the law.

- it is a dangerous practice, sometimes causing serious 'accidental' injuries or escalating into behaviour recognized as child **abuse**;
- it encourages violent attitudes and behaviour both in childhood and in later life – violence breeds violence;
- it teaches the world's children nothing positive.

37

Violence against oneself

Harming oneself is a kind of violence turned inwards. Self-harm includes not just suicide or suicide attempts, but deliberately cutting, burning or otherwise injuring oneself, abusing drugs or alcohol, and 'slimming' or starving oneself to the point of illness or death.

The cycle of violence

Self-harm can almost always be traced to deep emotional distress, often going back to childhood years. A high proportion of self-harmers have suffered **physical**, **emotional** or **sexual abuse** as children. Cutting or hurting themselves releases feelings of anger, anxiety and self-hatred. It can also mean the injured person receives attention and care, which may be otherwise lacking in their life. Self-harming is not necessarily linked to a desire to die.

Anorexia nervosa, 'the slimming disease'

Anorexia nervosa is an eating disorder that is far more serious than 'slimming that's got a bit out of hand'. Usually developing in adolescence, anorexia is a **psychological** disorder that creates an overpowering desire to be thin, and a genuine fear and disgust at the thought of being fat. A person with anorexia can see only a distorted, unrealistic image of their own body. They will eat less and less

> **FACT**
>
> *Eating disorders affect boys too – about 10% of anorexics are boys.*

An expression of distress – but the real scars are within for anorexic sufferers.

Between 90 to 95% of anorexics are female. Media images of super-thin models are sometimes blamed for influencing millions of girls who start to believe this is the 'ideal' body shape. Determined slimming to achieve such a figure can be the first step to anorexia.

ACTION

Anorexia and bulimia nervosa are serious conditions. If you feel you have an exaggerated desire to slim, or if you are worried about a friend, you should confide in a responsible adult.

Suicide attempts

Every year in the **developed world** thousands of people take their own life, and the numbers are increasing. Almost half have probably made suicide attempts before. Nearly three times more men than women kill themselves every year, and about five times more adolescent boys than girls. These figures might mean that more boys and men are attempting suicide, or that males tend to use more violent and successful methods, such as hanging, while females are more likely to use less reliable self-poisoning methods, such as an overdose of drugs. Each of these deaths is a sad testimony to loneliness and despair – and the waste of each individual's true potential.

or refuse food entirely. The wasting effect on their body can become increasingly extreme. They may begin to look just like pictures of famine victims with stick-like limbs, sunken features and loosened teeth. A woman's periods will probably stop, too. Some sufferers eventually die, unable to start eating even to save their own lives.

Bulimia nervosa is a related illness that about a third of anorexia sufferers develop. It involves binges, eating huge amounts of food, then making oneself sick to prevent putting on any weight.

FACT

In the UK in 1996, 3445 people died by suicide, several hundred more than were killed in road vehicle accidents in the same year.

The law

Most of the **developed world** has strict laws that protect the right to live without being subjected to violence by others. These laws are frequently broken, but their existence deters some violence and enables the police and others in the criminal justice system to arrest, detain and punish such law-breakers.

Children, violence and the law

Children are the focus of some separate laws because they are not able to defend or protect themselves, particularly from adults. These laws cover the general welfare of children and young people, as well as the responsibilities of their parents, guardians and indeed everyone, to safeguard children and respect their rights. Possible offences involving a child include neglect, cruelty, abandonment, exposure to risk or danger, assault and ill-treatment.

International laws and conventions

The United Nations (UN) is an organization working for peace and international co-operation. Almost all the countries in the world are members. It has many separate bodies within in it, including UNICEF (the United Nations International Children's Emergency Fund) and the UN High Commission for Refugees (UNHCR).

FACT

In the UK the Children and Young Persons Act (1933, 1969) and the Children Act (1989) are the laws that specifically protect children. The police, Social Services, Local Authorities and the National Society for the Prevention of Cruelty to Children (NSPCC) all have the power to take children out of situations where they are at risk or are actually being harmed, bring them to a safe place and start the legal process against those responsible.

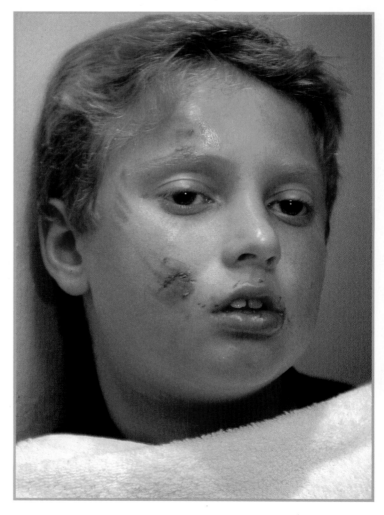

The United Nations Committee on the Rights of the Child is the highest international authority on the human rights of children. All but two countries in the world had signed up to the Convention on the Rights of the Child by 1997. It lays out many principles for protecting children from specific forms of violence and **abuse**, and also outlines ways of responding to violence by children.

Refining laws and guidelines

New laws and guidelines are being proposed and added all the time as governments and organizations worldwide recognize our wider responsibilities towards children.

Making sex tourists face the law

A growing number of nations are passing laws that mean anyone who visits a foreign country in order to have sex with children faces **prosecution** in their own country. Indeed, convicted child sex offenders might one day find it hard to travel abroad if it is thought that they pose a risk to children overseas.

An end to child soldiers? In 1998 UNICEF launched an international campaign to make recruiting children under 18 into the armed forces or sending children into any kind of combat a war crime.

41

What can I do?

Reading this book might make you feel there is so much violence in the world that nothing you can do would make a difference.

But everything you do can make a difference. **Non-violence** is not only an ideal to work towards, it is a state of mind and an attitude. Your school should be a violence-free zone and you can work towards making it one. Your home should be a place of safety – seek help if it is not because you may be the one person who can break the cycle. Look out for the people around you. Help them if they need it. Never be afraid to interfere unless you could be putting yourself at risk. Someone may be unable to ask for help, but may be able to accept it. If something worries you, talk about it. Violence thrives on silence and fear.

12 things you can do about violence

1 SAY NO!

If someone tries to hurt you or forces you to do something you know is wrong, say NO! Say it loudly, clearly and repeatedly.

2 BREAK THE SILENCE

If you are being hurt or know that someone else is being hurt by someone, tell an adult you can trust. Make it clear to people who ask you to keep secrets about violence that you won't.

3 DEMAND A BULLYING POLICY

Find out if your school has a policy about **bullying**. If it doesn't, get together with your classmates and teachers, talk to your head teacher or write to the board of governors at your school and demand a bullying policy.

4 DON'T STAND BY AND DO NOTHING

If others are being bullied or hurt, don't stand by and let it happen. Get help from an adult, stand up to bullies, tell the **victim** you want to help them. If it's a teacher bullying someone, get together with classmates, tell the head teacher and stand up to the bully.

5 BE A GOOD FRIEND

If you think a friend is a victim of bullying or **physical** or **sexual abuse**, try to talk about it with them. Even if it isn't a close friend, try to help – it could be you trying to cope alone. If you're scared of the **perpetrator** yourself, tell adults and let them tackle the problem.

6 BECOME A COUNSELLOR

Volunteer to become someone other children at school can turn to for advice and support. If there is no **counselling** project in your school, see if you can start one.

7 INTERFERE

If you think something's wrong, for example if a friend is in trouble or you're worried about how someone is treating a girlfriend or boyfriend, then interfere. Offer help, it might be needed, even if it can't be accepted straight away.

8 THINK FOR YOURSELF

Think about the issues. Work out for yourself what you really think about violence. Do you think it is wrong? Is violence ever necessary or justified? Inform yourself. Knowing what you believe and putting it in your own words is better than repeating things you have read but not really thought about.

9 WRITE ABOUT VIOLENCE

Find out the facts and write stories or articles for your school magazine, or produce a fact sheet on bullying or other kinds of violence. Write to your favourite magazines with your views on violence issues.

10 COMPLAIN

If you think a television programme was too violent or reinforced ideas of women and children as victims, write or phone in to complain.

11 LEARN SELF-DEFENCE

Learn self-defence or a martial art that will build your strength and physical confidence. Knowing how to defend yourself makes a difference to how you come across to others.

12 SUPPORT ORGANIZATIONS WORKING AGAINST VIOLENCE

Inform yourself about the work of different organizations and tell others about it. Join a local group, organize fund-raising events, or buy things from the organizations' shops and catalogues when you can.

Glossary

abuse wrong use, mistreatment or taking advantage

actual bodily harm a legal term describing physical injury

African National Congress (ANC) South African political party brought to power by Nelson Mandela

aggressive angry and unfriendly, seeming likely to attack

anonymous without giving a name

anorexia nervosa an illness where the sufferer starves to become unnaturally thin

apartheid separation of people of different races, usually white–black inequality

asylum safety or refuge given by one country to a person from another country

atrocities extremely cruel or wicked acts

bacteria tiny biological single-celled plants, some of which cause disease

bloodsport sports, such as hunting, that involve killing animals

bullying picking on someone physically, verbally or emotionally, or a serious, prolonged abuse of power

ChildLine a confidential UK help-and-advice-line for young victims of **bullying** or abuse

civilian person who is not in the army, navy or air force

civilized advanced in behaviour from a primitive or wild state

coercion forcing someone by pressure or persuasion to do something

colonization people from one country claiming control of another land

contaminated polluted, spoilt or no longer clean

counselling advice and support that helps people deal with personal or emotional problems

developed world countries with wealth and influence, achieved through industrialization and economic strength

developing world countries that are trying to improve their economic position, often by industrialization

ecological relating to plants, animals or the environment

eco warrior person who 'fights' to protect plants, animals or the environment

emotional abuse abuse that hurts someone mentally, frightens or threatens them, or deeply injures their feelings

ethnic group particular racial or cultural group

extreme/extremist going furthest, for example, being the most violent, having the strongest opinions

frustration feeling annoyed or upset when things do not go as expected or hoped

genetic related to the genes, inherited elements of human make-up

grieve go through the process of sorrow and loss when someone dies

hormone natural substance in animals and plants that has a physical effect when released into the blood stream or system

humiliation shame and deep embarrassment

injustice something that is not fair or is against someone's rights

Ku Klux Klan an extreme **racist** American organization for white Protestant supremacy

landmine bomb laid on or under the ground that goes off when stepped on

massacre cruel, violent killing, usually of a number of people

National Democratic Party in Burma, political party opposed to military control

Nazi German National Socialist, follower of Hitler, having extreme **racist** beliefs

negotiate work out something to suit both sides

non-violent not using violence or not believing in the use of violence

perpetrator the person who did a certain act, usually the person who committed a crime

persecution continually bothering or picking on others, hunting them down, even killing them

physical abuse mistreatment that hurts someone physically

prosecute in law, to take to court

psychiatric related to diseases of the mind

psychological related to the behaviour or workings of the mind

racist person who hates another race or believes one race is superior to another

radiation dangerous rays, particularly from a nuclear source

rape forced sex, forcing a person to have sex against their will

repeat victim someone who becomes a victim again and again

road rage anger or violence caused by annoying driving or traffic conditions

sexual abuse harmful mistreatment of someone in a sexual way

sexual assault harmful attack that involves sexual touching or forced sexual acts

social related to people, the community or society as a whole

street children rejected, deserted or orphaned children who survive however they can on the streets

terrorism organized use of violence or threats to force a government or organization to do something

torture causing terrible pain or mental suffering to someone, usually as a punishment

unethical against or less than an accepted moral standard

victim person subjected to pain, ill-treatment, suffering or death

violation breaking or ignoring a law, promise or agreement

virus a tiny living particle that can infect a plant or animal with disease

Contacts and helplines

AMNESTY INTERNATIONAL

99 Roseberry Avenue, London EC1R 4RE
0171 814 6200 – Children's & Youth network
and information on international campaigns

CHILDLINE

General enquiries/project information
Royal Mail Building, Studd Street
London N1 0QW, *0171 239 1000*
24–hour freephone helpline *0800 1111*;
http://www.childline.org.uk

Childline Scotland

Bullying freephone line open Monday to Friday
3.30–9.30 pm *0800 441111* – Help and advice
about violence, abuse, problems at home. For
letters requesting support and advice:
ChildLine, Freepost 1111, London N1 0BR

THE CHILDREN'S SOCIETY

Edward Rudolf House, Margery Street
London, WC1X 0JL, *0171 837 4299* – Helping
children on the streets, in prisons or excluded
from school

EATING DISORDERS ASSOCIATION

Sackville Place, 44–48 Magdalen Street,
Norwich, Norfolk, NR3 1JU
Helpline *01603 621414* – Advice about
anorexia and other eating problems

EPOCH WORLDWIDE (End Physical Punishment of Children)

77 Holloway Road, London N7 8JZ
0171 700 0627 – Campaign to stop smacking
and other forms of physical punishment

EVERYMAN CENTRE

30 Brixton Road, London SW9 6BU
0171 793 0255 – Working on violence issues
with schools and the black community,
particularly with boys

KIDSCAPE

152 Buckingham Palace Road, London SW1
9TR, *0171 730 3300* – Campaigns, information
and advice about children's safety, Helpline
Monday and Wednesday 9.30–5.00 pm
0171 730 3300

NATIONAL SELF-HARM NETWORK

c/o Survivors Speak Out, 34 Osnaburgh Street
London NW1 3ND, *0171 916 5472* –
Advice and support for self-harmers

NSPCC (National Society for the Prevention of Cruelty to Children)

National Centre, Curtain Road
London, EC2A 3NH, *0171 825 2500* –
Protecting children from cruelty, danger and
violence

THE SAMARITANS

10 The Grove, Slough, SL1 1QP
01753 532713 – Confidential helplines for
any problem, including suicidal feelings

SAVE THE CHILDREN FUND

17 Grove Land, London, SE5 8RD
0171 703 5400 – National and international
campaigns around children's issues

UNICEF (United Nations International Children's Emergency Fund)

UK Committee, 55 Lincoln's Inn Fields
London WC2A 3NB, *0171 405 5592*
Children's welfare committee

In Australia, use the following contacts:

SAVE THE CHILDREN, AUSTRALIA

PO Box 1281, Collingwood 3066

VICTIMS REFERRAL AND ASSISTANCE SERVICE

GPO Box 4356 QQ, Melbourne, VIC 3001
(03) 9603 9797 – Helpline **1800 819 817**

NATIONAL CAMPAIGN AGAINST VIOLENCE AND CRIME

http:// www.ncavac.gov.au – Information and
advice

KIDS HELPLINE

1800 551800 – Freecall for advice and support

REACH OUT

http://www.reachout.asu.au – Resource for
young people going through tough times

Further reading

Fiction

Bully
Yvonne Coppard
Red Fox, 1991

Hillsden Riots/Getting it Wrong
Rhodri Jones
André Deutsch, 1991 (Adlib series)

We All Fall Down
Robert Cormier
Victor Gollancz, 1992

Rocky and the Black-eye Mystery
Sylvia Sherry
Jonathan Cape, 1992

That was Then, This is Now
S E Hinton
Lion, 1993

Underworld III
Peter Beere
Hippo, 1992

The Bullies Meet the Willow Street Kids
Michelle Elliott
Pan Macmillan, 1993

The War of Jenkins Ear
Michael Mopurgo
Mammoth, 1994

Children's Ward – On the Run
Helen White
BBC, 1993

Cold Blood
Alan Durant
Fantail, 1994

The Dead Are Listening
Francis McCrickard
Spindlewood, 1995

Riot
Peter Beere
Hippo, 1994

Runner
Elizabeth Hawkin
Orchard Books, 1997

Watsons Go To Birmingham
Christopher Paul Curtis
Orion, 1997

Weirdo's War
Michael Coleman
Orchard Books, 1998

Lost for Words
Elizabeth Lutzier
Macmillan, 1993

Ticket to Freedom
Rosemary Harris
Faber & Faber, 1995

Tina Come Home
Paul Geraghty
Red Fox, 1994

Non-fiction

My Body is Private
Linda Walvoord Girard
Albert Whitman, 1984

We're Talking about Bullying
Anne Charlish
Wayland, 1997

Dealing with Bullying
Yvette Solomon, John Coleman
Wayland, 1998

Hitting People is Wrong – and children are people too
Radda Barnen
Epoch Worldwide, 1994

Rights in the Home, (What do we mean by human rights?)
Emma Haughton
Franklin Watts, 1997

Feeling Violent (What do you know about ...?)
Pete Sanders
Franklin Watts, 1994

No Easy Walk to Freedom
Nelson Mandela (autobiography)
Heinemann Educational Books, 1990

Index